Willow's Day

Repairing Harm and Building Bridges

The Art of Apologising and Accepting an Apology

by Ge... Benger and Caryn Price

I0559937

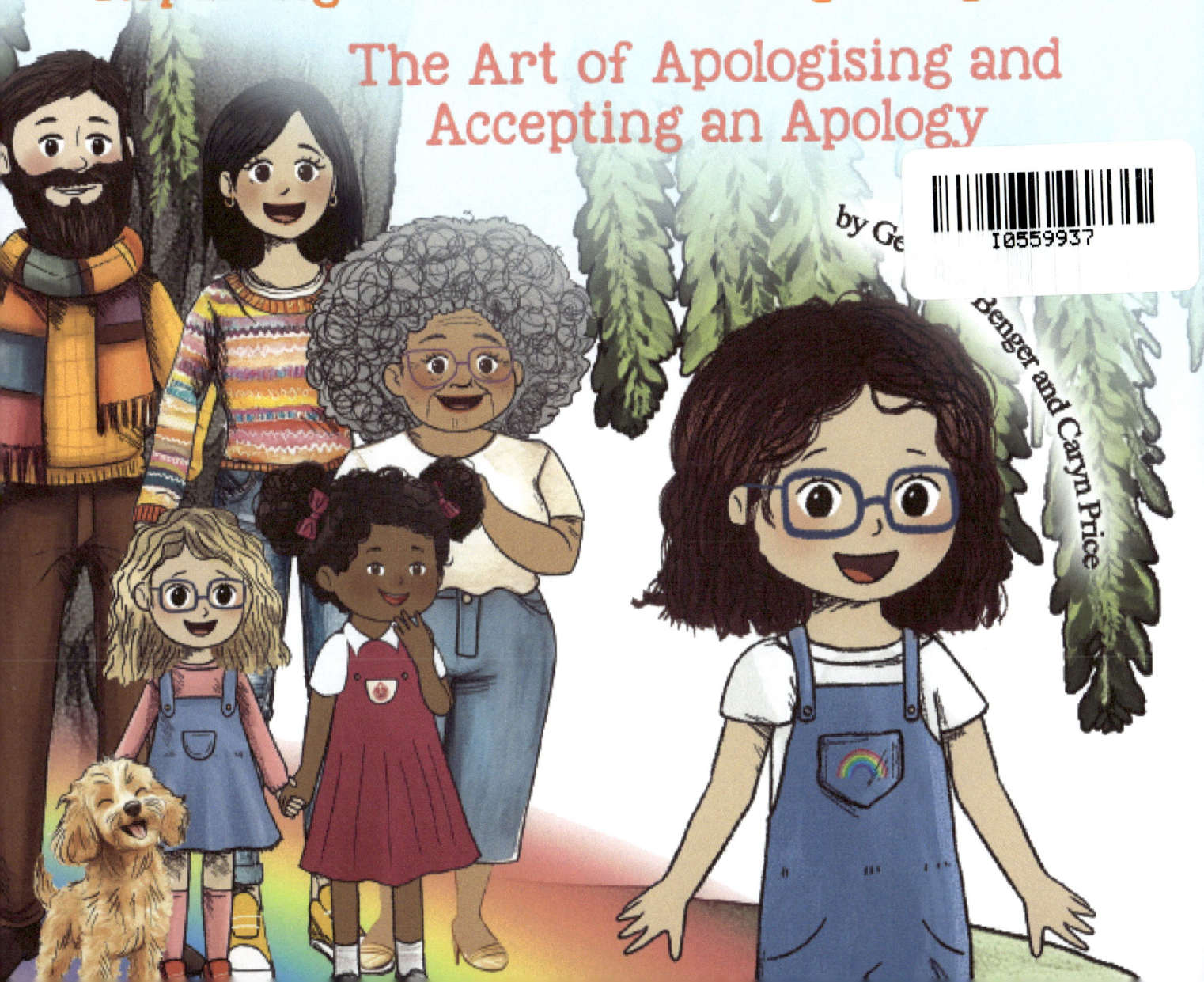

Willow's Day

Repairing Harm & Building Bridges
The Art of Apologising and Accepting an Apology

by Georgina Benger and Caryn Price

Copyright © Caryn Price and Georgina Benger 2025
All rights reserved.

No part of this publication may be reproduced, distributed, or transmitted in any form or by any means, including photocopying, recording, or other electronic or mechanical methods, without the authors' prior written permission, except in the case of brief quotations embodied in critical reviews and certain other non-commercial uses permitted by copyright law.

For permission requests, please get in touch with the authors.

Acknowledgments

A heartfelt thank you to our parents, whose love and guidance have shaped our understanding of kindness and empathy. Your unwavering support means everything to us. We are so grateful for your guidance on the importance of sincerity in giving and accepting apologies.

Dedication

For all the children and adults discovering the power of "I'm sorry" and the grace of accepting an apology. May you always be able to repair hearts and build bridges in your relationships with authenticity.

About the Authors

Georgina Benger and Caryn Price are mothers and passionate advocates for education, each bringing years of experience and qualifications to their work. The most notable of these are Caryn's two Master's degrees, specialising in psychology and inclusivity, and Georgina's Master of Education from Cambridge, focusing on restorative justice in childhood relationships. Together, they combine their expertise to inspire a more inclusive and compassionate approach to holistic learning for both children and educators.

This is the story of Willow's day...

Willow's head is full of creative ideas, and her heart is full of inquisitiveness—a wonderful combination!

Willow loves stacking stones and eating cereal without milk!

She loves going to the beach with her friend, Olive, and she most especially loves drawing rainbows.

The most perfect thing, to Willow's mind, is drawing rainbows with Olive.

Willow's second most perfect thing is eating chocolate biscuit cake, which is sticky and crunchy. It has no biscuits in it, but all the end-of-packet breakfast cereals.

But, of course, her ultimate favourite thing is drawing rainbows with Olive while savouring every bite of that delicious cake!

Willow has many friends and lovely teachers at Pomegranate Road Primary School, which is just two front doors away from her home!

This means Willow can walk to school every single day with her sister, Freya, and her loyal, energetic, and fluffy dog, Mabel.

Even if it's snowing, nothing stops Willow from getting to class!

One sunny Friday, it was Willow's Design and Technology class. She was super excited! They were finally making their 3D bridges.

Everyone was busy. Willow had decided to build hers out of construction bricks. She had spent weeks digging all the yellow bricks out of the giant construction boxes at home and at school. She had practised her ideas in her drawings. She had dreamt of the moment she would be placing her final piece, but she was particularly excited about taking her bridge home and showing it to her Grandma.

Willow's Grandma was an engineer, and Willow loved hearing her stories about what she was designing!

The children had spent all morning building. It was hard work, but fun.

Before the break, Mr Beech said, "Time to go and wash your hands; let's get ready for lunchtime."

As the children bustled out, Dido tripped and kicked Willow's bridge, which caved in on the left-hand side.

Willow was shocked! She couldn't believe her eyes and burst into tears. The tears were hot on her cheeks, and her hands scrunched into fists. She then felt furious!

"You ruined my bridge! You did it on purpose! You broke my whole bridge!"

Feeling embarrassed and frustrated, Willow angrily wailed to her teacher, "Mr Beech! She's ruined it all."

Mr Beech was helping Alfie zip up his coat; it seemed he hadn't heard Willow.

Willow lashed out at the nearest bridge, angrily hitting it to the floor.

Dido shouted out.

Mr Beech calmly appeared, took both of their hands, and walked them away from the models.

"You are both such good friends; I know we can repair all of this harm," Mr Beech whispered.

Mr Beech was quiet. Dido and Willow were not. The class could hear the same shouty words from both girls, all about who had done what.

Their voices got louder while Mr Beech's got quieter.

As the class walked off to lunch, Mr Beech asked Willow and Dido to draw the harm that was so fresh in their minds. He reminded them that this safe space was a time for them to listen to each other and share their perspectives of the event.

Willow loved to draw, and as she replayed what had just happened, she drew the accident. For that was what it was. An accident...

But Willow had not accidentally punched Dido's model. Willow had felt very, very sad — and then very, very angry.

Mr Beech explained that feeling shocked, feeling sad, feeling furious, feeling embarrassed, and feeling frustrated were all natural human emotions. He even said that sometimes he felt those feelings too!

In fact, that very morning, he had felt angry and frustrated about Mr Ash chipping his new coffee cup!

Mr. Beech asked the girls to repair the harm done. He explained that all feelings are valid, but not all behaviours are acceptable.

Willow and Dido looked down, then at each other, and instantly blurted out, "SORRY," together.

Willow said, "I am sorry, Dido, for breaking your model."
Dido replied, "Thank you for your apology."

They then laughed so loudly that even Mr Beech joined in as they walked back to lunch, Mr Beech told the girls that they should feel proud of themselves. They had helped each other to understand what had gone wrong, and they had rebuilt their friendship — and their models.

During the afternoon break, Willow and Jake played together, as they always did. However, today things went unexpectedly, and badly, wrong.

Willow accidentally bumped Jake too hard, causing him to misstep and fall to the ground. Everyone laughed at him.

Feeling hurt and embarrassed, Jake jumped to his feet, his cheeks reddening with anger.

"You always do this, Willow! You just want to win, so you pushed me!" he shouted.

Shocked by his reaction, Willow felt guilt wash over her.

"I'm really sorry, Jake! I didn't mean to hurt you," she responded, but Jake was too upset to listen. He turned away, crossed his arms, and stomped off to sit on the picnic bench.

Willow recognised that she had upset her friend but felt worried because she didn't know how to repair the harm.

Luckily, Mr Beech was on duty. He had seen it all happen and knew that many problems are caused by miscommunication.

Mr Beech said, "Willow, well done for apologising to Jake. I saw you say sorry. Jake is on the bench and is sitting with his feelings for a moment."

After they had given Jake some space, Mr Beech explained to Willow how and why Jake might be feeling different emotions.

Willow now understood more. So, she decided to approach Jake. "Jake," she said, her heart racing. Jake looked uneasy but nodded. "I'm really sorry for bumping you too hard. I didn't mean to hurt you. I got carried away in the game."

Jake was quiet, so Mr Beech stepped in to help.

He gently guided Jake on how to respond, encouraging him to acknowledge Willow's apology and express his feelings. He also reminded Jake that Willow had taken responsibility for her actions, which was important.

And so, Willow and Jake sat together on the bench for a while, talking things through. They ended their day with their friendship repaired, and their feelings finally understood.

Willow and Freya skipped home, desperate to see Mabel, their dog. They bundled through the front door, and Mabel greeted them with licks.

Willow ran through to show Grandma her bridge. Grandma loved it!

Mum called them all to the table for their cheesy pasta and broccoli. They all chatted about their different day.

Then Mum noticed that Willow had eaten every single morsel... her plate was totally empty!

"Wow, Willow, you should feel so proud for eating all of your broccoli! I know you don't really like it, so I'm really pleased!" Willow felt happy for a flash; she loved hearing her Mum say that.

"I ate it all!" said Willow.

But then, Willow felt a sense of panic and guilt, and her heart started to race. She went slightly pink. She looked out at the rain on the windowpane.

Willow had not eaten her broccoli. Willow had given it to Freya.

Freya stared at Willow; Willow stared back.

Mum got some ice cream from the freezer and said they could watch TV together before bath time.

Suddenly, Willow blurted out, "I didn't eat it."

She almost shouted the words. She had to get them out. And then she burst into tears.

Willow now looked at her Mum. Her Mum looked at her. Freya looked at Willow and then at her Mum.

Mum sat back at the table and said, "Tell me about the broccoli, Willow."

Willow explained that she hated broccoli more than anything in the world — even more than the dark and Freya loved it so much that she had given it to her.

Mum nodded and said, "It's hard to eat things we don't like. It's okay to feel that way."

She added, "But when you said you ate it, I believed you."

Willow snuggled into her Mum, feeling so sad. As her Mum hugged her back, she said, "How about apologising for being dishonest?"

"I'm sorry I lied, Mum. I was scared you'd be cross with me," Willow whispered.

Mum thanked Willow for her apology and said, "Instead of avoiding the issue, let's brainstorm together about what you think could have been done differently."

Mum paused for a few seconds, allowing Willow to think about what she had just said, and then asked, "Can we find a compromise?"

They figured out that Willow didn't mind the treetop bit of the broccoli. She really hated the trunk bit. They all agreed she could eat the top bits and leave the trunks.

Mum finished the chat with a hug and said, "I really appreciate it when you're honest with me, Willow — even when it's hard to tell the truth. It helps us to work things out together better. We trust each other, but that trust can be harmed when we lie."

Mum turned on the TV.

Willow grabbed her pens and paper; she sat and mindfully drew one of the best rainbow drawings she'd ever done. It was for her Mum, and it was the biggest sorry of her day.

At the end of the evening, Mum checked in with Willow, asking if there was anything else she wanted to share. Willow just wanted a hug and her usual bedtime.

It had been a super sorry day, but Willow closed her eyes, hugged Mabel, and knew that she could repair harm and rebuild her friendships.

Tomorrow was a new day — full of possibilities!

She had learnt that apologising and accepting apologies allowed kindness and understanding into her life — and that made her really happy.

Understanding Restorative Justice at Home: What Everyone Raising Children Should Know

Restorative justice is a compassionate, relationship-focused approach that helps young children understand the impact of their actions and learn to repair harm. Whether your child has told a lie, hurt someone's feelings, or broken a rule, this method fosters emotional growth, accountability, and empathy.

Here are seven key steps to help you practise restorative justice at home:

Create a Safe Space
Why it matters:
Start by creating a calm, non-judgemental environment. Avoid reacting with anger or punishment. Sit at your child's level, speak gently, and make sure they feel physically and emotionally safe enough to open up. A peaceful space builds trust and makes meaningful reflection possible.

Listen Actively
What to do:
Invite your child to share what happened in their own words. Use open-ended questions such as, "Can you tell me what happened?" "What happened next?" or "Can you tell me more about that?" Show you're listening through eye contact, gentle nods, or by repeating back what they've said. Allow them to draw if words are difficult. Avoid interrupting or correcting—this is their chance to be heard.

Acknowledge Their Emotions
Why it helps:
Children need to feel that their emotions are valid. Say things such as, "It must have felt really frustrating," or "I can see that scared you." Helping them to name their feelings—such as embarrassment, anger, jealousy, or disappointment—builds emotional intelligence and reduces shame or defensiveness.

Explore the Impact
What you might ask:
Guide your child gently to think about how their actions may have affected others. Ask, "How do you think your friend felt when that happened?" This helps them develop empathy and understand the ripple effects of their choices.

Encourage Accountability
What it looks like:
Support your child in taking responsibility without blame. Rather than forcing an apology, ask, "What could you do to help make things better?" or "What could you do next time?" Offer ideas if they need support, but give them the space to take the lead in making amends.

Facilitate a Dialogue
When others are involved:
If another person was affected and it feels appropriate, bring them into the conversation. Help both sides share how they felt and listen to one another. Act as a calm, neutral guide to ensure everyone feels heard and respected.

Solutions and Follow-Up
What comes next:

Work together to come up with a way to repair the harm—saying sorry for the action, writing a note, helping fix something, or making a kind gesture. Later, check in with your child: "How are things going now?" or "Do you feel things are better?"

Always acknowledge their effort to make things right. Restorative justice isn't about perfection—it's about building trust, growing empathy, and deepening relationships over time.

Understanding Restorative Justice in the Classroom: What Every Teacher Should Know

Restorative justice is a compassionate, relationship-based approach that helps children understand the impact of their actions and supports them in making things right. Whether a child has disrupted the class, hurt a peer's feelings, or broken a rule, restorative practices promote emotional growth, empathy, and accountability while strengthening the classroom community.

Here are seven key steps to help you practise restorative justice effectively in your classroom:

Create a Safe Space
Why it matters:
Step away from the rest of the class if possible. Speak in a soft, non-judgemental tone and ensure the child feels safe to talk. Avoid punishment or public correction—this moment is about connection, not consequence.

Listen Actively
What to do:
Invite the child to explain what happened, using open-ended prompts such as, "Can you help me understand what happened?" or "I'm here to listen; what led up to this?" Use eye contact, calm body language, and paraphrasing to show you're listening. Allow them to draw or write if verbal expression is difficult.

Acknowledge Emotions
Why it helps:
Children need to feel that their emotions are valid. Validating their emotions fosters self-awareness and reduces shame, which can otherwise block reflection. Say things such as, "It must have felt really frustrating," or "I can see that scared you." Helping them to name their feelings—such as embarrassment, anger, jealousy, or disappointment—builds emotional intelligence and reduces defensiveness.

Explore the Impact
What you might ask:
Gently guide the child to consider how their behaviour affected others. Ask, "How do you think your classmate felt when that happened?" This helps them connect actions to consequences and encourages empathy.

Encourage Accountability
What it looks like:
Support children in taking ownership of their actions without blame. Replace forced apologies with genuine reflection: "What do you think you can do to make this right?" Provide support if needed, but allow them to take the lead.

Facilitate a Dialogue
If others are involved:

When appropriate, bring together the individuals affected. Help each person express how they felt and listen to the other. Your role is to guide gently, keeping the focus on understanding and restoring connection, not blame.

Solutions and Follow-Up
What comes next:

Support children in thinking of ways to repair the harm—saying sorry for the action, writing a kind note, or offering help. Then revisit the situation later: "How are things going now?" or "Do you feel things have improved?"

Celebrate honesty, reflection, and effort. Restorative justice isn't about being perfect—it's about restoring trust, rebuilding responsibility, and reconnecting relationships.

Further Reading

Augustine, C. H., Engberg, J., Grimm, G. E., Lee, E., Lin Wang, E., Christianson, K., & Joseph, A. A. (2018). Can restorative practices improve school climate and curb suspensions? An evaluation of the impact of restorative practices in a mid-sized urban school district. Santa Monica, CA: Rand Corporation.

Benger, G. (2023, July 29). A reflection, and small-scale study, exploring transforming conflict resolution practice by employing an approach rooted in a restorative justice pedagogy (Master's dissertation). Faculty of Education, University of Cambridge.

Cantor, P., Osher, D., Berg, J., Steyer, L., & Rose, T. (2019). Malleability, plasticity, and individuality: How children learn and develop in context. Applied Developmental Science, 23(4), 307–337. https://-doi.org/10.1080/10888691.2017.1398649

Coakley, A. (2020). Peer mediation – conflict management in a class of its own. Journal of Mediation & Applied Conflict Analysis, 6(2).

Coleman, P. T., Deutsch, M., & Marcus, E. C. (2014). The handbook of conflict resolution: Theory and practice (3rd ed.). San Francisco, CA: Jossey-Bass.

Cremin, H. (2007). Peer mediation: Citizenship and social inclusion revisited: Citizenship and social inclusion in action. London: McGraw-Hill Education (UK).

Cremin, H., & Bevington, T. (2017). Positive peace in schools: Tackling conflict and creating a culture of peace in the classroom. Abingdon: Routledge.

Davidson, J., & Wood, C. (2004). A conflict resolution model. Theory Into Practice, 43(1), 6–13. A Conflict Resolution Model

Grolnick, W. S. (2009). The role of parents in facilitating autonomous self-regulation for education. Theory and Research in Education, 7(2), 164–173. The role of parents in facilitating autonomous self-regulation for education - Wendy S. Grolnick, 2009

MacDiarmid, L. (2024). Apology–forgiveness in restorative justice: Victims' experiences with justice-involved youth. Probation Journal. Advance online publication. Apology–forgiveness in restorative justice: Victims' experiences with justice-involved youth - Laura MacDiarmid, 2025

Rahim, M. A. (2011). Managing conflict in organisations. Piscataway, NJ: Transaction Publishers.

Rahim, M. A., & Bonoma, T. V. (1979). Managing organizational conflict: A model for diagnosis and intervention. Psychological Reports, 44(3, Pt 2), 1323–1344. https://doi.org/10.2466/pr0.1979.44.3c.1323

Vygotsky, L. S. (1978). Mind in society: The development of higher psychological processes. Cambridge, MA: Harvard University Press.

Zehr, H. (2002). The little book of restorative justice. Intercourse, PA: Good Books.

Willow's Day
Repairing Harm and Building Bridges

Willow's day started like any other, but soon spiralled into what she calls a "super sorry day."

One misunderstanding led to another, and before long, feelings were hurt and everything felt a little tangled. Willow was left feeling gloomy and stuck.
With the gentle guidance of her Mum, the kindness of her teacher Mr Beech, and the steady wisdom of Granny, an engineer who builds bridges, Willow begins to find her way through. Together, they help her talk about her feelings, listen with care, and take brave steps to mend what was broken. Along the way Willow learns that saying sorry with honesty, and accepting apologies with compassion, can build stronger relationships.

This engaging and accessible book is a valuable resource for educators, parents and children, introducing the foundational practices of restorative justice in a simple, child-friendly way. It gently guides readers in exploring empathy, emotional repair, responsibility and accountability— offering a thoughtful first step towards healing harm and moving beyond traditional punishment.

Featuring a dyslexia-friendly font and colour-coded pages to support emotional regulation and accessible reading.

Pomegranate
Education
Rooted in lived experience.
Informed by research.

£12.99

www.ingramcontent.com/pod-product-compliance
Lightning Source LLC
Chambersburg PA
CBHW041435120626
46547CB00002B/230

* 9 7 8 1 9 6 8 9 6 6 5 3 9 *